Healing Your Scars

Getting Past Your Break-up

Kimberly Christian

TABLE OF CONTENT

INTRODUCTION

I'm aware that you might be experiencing a lot of grief, hurt, and disappointment right now. I've been there a lot of times. And I'm certain that you have very good reasons for feeling the way you do. I'm sure I did.

I'm also certain that you are experiencing some sense of loss, whether you ended the relationship or the other person did. I know of the harm that may have been caused in and by the relationship, I believe it is quite normal for us to experience these emotions when we part ways with someone we hold dear.

However, just because it's time to move on doesn't mean you have to forget about that individual. It just means continuing on with what comes after, and it seems preferable to decide to do so forcefully.

And why, you ask, should you do this? My best response is that it's now all about YOU in your life. This is now YOUR LIFE to live, regardless of the reason you are no longer together.The focus has shifted from the other person to your happiness, healing, and fulfillment—not what your friends or family may think.

You are FREE after you have genuinely moved on from a situation and someone. You are free to live fully, pain-free, and, if you so desire, open up to someone else. On the other side, if you do not truly move on from your previous relationship(s) and recover, you will unavoidably invite additional suffering.

When we are not fully healed, the measures we attempt to protect our wounds can and often do leave others perplexed and increase our own suffering.You will find proof to back up your dread of getting injured again if you have not entirely recovered from the past. I believe that we have all been in a relationship with someone who is carrying ancient wounds, and those wounds have a very negative impact on the current relationship. Both sides may find this to be highly aggravating.

CHAPTER 1 The Truth About Break-up

It's over now,

"We should speak."

"It's me, not you," he said.

"I believe we need a break."

Let's be honest. A relationship cannot be ended in a polite manner. Every time a relationship ends, parts of you are lost, leaving only a hollow behind. Emotions that make you feel as though you will be fully swallowed up and lost exist in that gap. You might notice that you're starting to withdraw a bit and don't want to get out of bed. When the person who played a crucial role in your life is no longer present, who wants to get out of bed and face the world?

I was one of those people who thought that when my first love left me, my life had come to an end. We lived in the same flatwe collaborated. A few days before Valentine's Day, he broke up with me.

What was his justification? He claimed that the chemistry we shared at the beginning of our relationship had faded. | was distraught, i sobbed nonstop. We still shared a home and continued to work together, which made the process of moving on quite challenging. The sexual activity continued. We discussed reconciling once more. There were even references to getting married.

Now that's where my healing process was wrong,I couldn't heal,I couldn't set the necessary boundaries that were needed in every break-up. We were still active sexually and unlike him I had hope of getting back with him,but then the hope was lost when one day he got a lease on the apartment.

In our world of romance, heartbreak is a sad but frequently inescapable situation. Few people are able to maintain a single relationship for the remainder of their life, and even fewer are able to marry the first person they date. Being in a partnership might help you achieve wonderful things, but if you wind up parting ways with the person you believed would be your lifelong partner, the grief of separation will be much harder to handle. If the relationship you shared was problematic or even poisonous, this situation is made worse, making it even harder than usual to move on.

However, it's important to keep in mind that even if your relationship has ended, you shouldn't end up failing too. Unfortunately, not everyone uses this information in their work.Since the sadness associated with a breakup can be difficult, they are not to blame. The fact is that you have lost someone and something you genuinely believed in.

Again, it's crucial to keep in mind that breakups aren't always the same and aren't always simple throughout this time. Depending on the terms of the agreement, you could not have been allowed to see your ex again or you might have chosen to maintain contact. Or You might have to work together every day or just once a week when it's time for you to return each other's possessions. Know of how your breakup plays out, you can be sure that it will be a trying time. You'll consequently feel a variety of emotions during your breakup phase, as you've probably noticed. You can go back and forth between different emotions, such as anger and melancholy, disappointment and self-doubt. These feelings are all normal during a breakup. However, how we handle those emotions affects how long we endure pain and how much it affects us. In a similar vein, how we handle our emotions affects how quickly we bounce back. Fortunately, there are techniques to protect yourself from further suffering. There are strategies for overcoming sadness. You can maintain your self-respect and dignity in a number of ways. Although a breakup may initially feel overwhelming, your pain will pass and you will heal.

A breakup does not guarantee that you will never fall in love again or that you will always feel this depressed. The loss of a relationship is not the end of the world, despite what it may seem like, and you shouldn't stop living your life or take severe measures like giving up on finding love again. Even though this moment in your life may be challenging, if you put your attention on healing, you may come out of it with a revitalized sense of self-love, a more upbeat outlook, and a greater understanding of yourself.

To let go of someone you once had feelings for or still have feelings for is difficult. You may have started to think about your goals for the future and your relationships. However, if you are still carrying around emotional burdens from a prior relationship, it may be difficult to avoid dwelling on the past.

A relationship's termination might still have an effect on us years later. It can be difficult to accept that something that was once a very important component of your life is now just a memory. Similarly, if there are unresolved issues, it could be difficult to admit that the relationship has ended at all.

So Yes,that's the truth about break ups,you get to leave a large part of you with that person and if not healed properly YOU could actually lose it. It's frightening,I know,but that's why you have me,that's why you have this book. To journey with me in your process of healing,it will take months, sometimes years,but knowing the right healing methods with this book,you can be sure of wanting to TRY again.

CHAPTER 2 Understanding Your Breakup

The pain of a lost love that lingers like a stealthy poison is something we've all experienced at some point.

It is impossible to imagine what life would be like without them in it. Some people who are severely depressed lose the motivation to lead fulfilled lives or, worse yet, commit crimes. It's difficult to let go of a loved one, and I want to help you feel understood. Regardless of whether you're still reeling from the end of a stormy long-distance relationship, trying to forget someone who betrayed you, or simply attempting to move on from a toxic relationship, we understand.

When someone is vague with you about the reasons they choose to end the relationship, it can be difficult to understand the reasons why after a traumatic breakup. In other words, your ex won't tell you the specific causes of the split. However, it is virtually always evident that your ex was no longer content with your relationship.Furthermore, we have discovered that their decision to split up was typically also unavoidable. On the other hand, you can think that everything is fine and that the relationship is going well. Let's explore the reasons for a breakup and attempt to explain this difference in viewpoint in this post.

Recognize the actual problems that caused your separation.

Did your ex ever compliment you on who you are as a person? that despite the fact that they are unable to be with you, you deserve all the happiness in the world? After a breakup, many people still feel the urge to "guard" their former. Simply put, they feel bad about their choice and do not want you to suffer even more as a result.

They aren't honest about the real problems they were having when they were with you. If you believe this to be the case, attempt to concentrate on identifying the precise reasons why the relationship ended. To solve the issue, you must identify its source. You will then be in a position to address the problem. Knowing this will help you to appreciate how important it is to keep up a cordial relationship with your ex. Don't engage them in confrontation or wait for them to voluntarily express their true feelings to you on your terms. It is safe to argue that you have not fully understood the repercussions associated with your breakup until you act with this objective in mind and thoroughly comprehend why.

You understand that it is challenging to embrace the possibility of your relationship ending abruptly one day. On its own, this can cause a great deal of tension and anxiety, but when you don't know why the relationship ended, the situation can get much worse. However, it is essential to make an effort to maintain a cheerful attitude. You will need to make yourself cheer up whether your final objective is to get back together or even just to move on. The best approach to not only get over the breakup but also comprehend its causes is to have a positive outlook.I will advise you to write a handwritten letter to your ex if nothing else seems to be working and you're dealing with someone who won't listen to your need to know what actually transpired. You should be able to move on and imagine a new, better relationship together after finally understanding the reasons for your separation.We cannot emphasize enough how important it is to conduct this brainstorming session in writing. Please don't hesitate to grab a pen and paper and begin right away by noting anything your ex has said in previous conversations or instances where they may have gotten angry at you. Please finish this before you write the letter by hand. This aspect of planning is an essential step in discovering the real reasons behind the separation.

You are inherently more exact and honest with yourself while going through such an exercise and holding yourself accountable by writing your thoughts down. Once more, this is only a step in the action-preparation process called analysis. Finally, using the knowledge you have gained, you will write a handwritten letter to that person in order to understand what is really going through his or her mind. Making a connection between your mistakes, your ex's expectations, and the split will be crucial in this letter. With the newfound knowledge, you will be able to complete this activity as efficiently as possible.

So With all this,it's important to actually know what went wrong in your relationship, knowing your flaws go a long way. It also helps in building your relationship life,you won't possibly make a mistake twice,you learn and relearn.

CHAPTER 3 The Grieving Stage

It's never easy to see the person who broke your heart walk out the door. You could feel as though your stomach is in knots and you have no idea what it's like to be single. Self-reflection and other methods could help you start to feel the weight of your crushed heart lifting.

We do not naturally know how to let go of things. There is an unmistakable art to moving on, one that we are continuously relearning in a culture that encourages us to hold onto what we love at all costs.

The Grieving Process After a Breakup

Breaking up is difficult. It takes time for wounds to heal after a breakup, whether it be with a boyfriend, girlfriend, husband, life partner, or even the closest friend. There are five phases of grieving that you will go through, regardless of who sensed the split. According to Mental-Health-Matters, they are denial, rage, bargaining, depression, and acceptance.

Denial

According to "How to Survive the Five Steps of Grief after a Breakup," denial is your brain's default reaction to unwelcome news. Denial offers your heart some time to get used to the new circumstances. You can believe that your significant other is approaching you during the denial period. The denial stage lasts for varying lengths of time for each person. It is a good idea to ask your friends and family for assistance.

Anger

According to the website Mental-Health-Matters, it's acceptable to be angry at your ex-partner. You may hold grudges against her for hurting you or dissolving your family. Avoid making any hasty decisions that you might later regret at this phase. Wait till you're less emotional.

Bargaining

During the negotiation stage, you'll work to mend fences and possibly start over as friends. According to Relationship Life Tips, this could have disastrous results. The website serves as a reminder to those who are hurt that romantic relationships contain features that don't go away right away. In the immediate aftermath of a split, trying to reconnect with an ex will only make the pain of heartbreak worse. By reestablishing yourself without your ex, you can destroy your pride.

Depression

Being depressed is common. According to Mental-Health-Matters, at this stage of grief, you accept the reality that nothing will change. Now is the time to think. You may prefer to be alone. Recognize that people's goodwill is not meant to offend you. Find a support system,it helps trust me.

Acceptance

It's normal to have a special space in your heart for your family. Particular relationships shape who you are. However, you will start to piece together what happened, accept the breakup, and recognise your role in it in the final stage of sorrow following a breakup. suggests taking advantage of this chance to reflect on past errors and carry lessons learned into the future. This is the best method to move on after a breakup and become a stronger person. Even if the agony might not quite be gone yet, the wounds will eventually mend.

The pain of a breakup may be unrelenting, even if your broken heart tries to tell you it's for the best and your sad and foggy head assures you it will pass. It's important to take your time when getting over a breakup; it's your time to reflect, recharge, and learn from the experience. But what if your healing could be complete and strong... and quicker? Maybe science just found the answer.

CHAPTER 4   10 Ways To Let Go

Whether we are aware of it or not, relationships have a significant impact on the self-perceptions we hold. Being 'intertwined' with a spouse is quite typical within a relationship. Goals, directions, and wants and requirements for the now and the future all change. This isn't because you lose yourself, though it might happen, but rather because intimacy requires opening yourself to the love, needs, wants, opinions, feelings, and ambitions and dreams of the other person. You can't help but be influenced when something occurs, and you finally end yourself moving in the same way. Occasionally, this entails adjusting your own sails. All of this is a normal aspect of being fully with someone and a part of the illogical magic of relationships.

The undoing of this union, which is terrible to go through, is what a breakup entails. The breakdown of a relationship can also result in the breakdown of a person's self-concept, regardless of how resilient and independent they may be. The upheaval of your familiar routines is one of the most difficult aspects of a breakup. The familiar is gone, plans are altered, and the future suddenly has an excessive amount of empty places where joyful things formerly were.

1.   Talk About It!

There are a few ways that discussing a breakup could aid in the healing process. The first is that discussing the relationship will assist to view things from a different angle. It's a good thing it's not dubbed a "breakup" because it's working. Being in love or having a lot of likes can sometimes muddle, conceal, and dress up things at the expense of clarity.When you discuss the relationship from a more dispassionate standpoint, a level of insight will suddenly appear at your feet.

2.   Locate Your Tale

Talking makes it easier to create a narrative about the relationship that offers meaning to the experience, including the dating, the breakup, and—possibly most significantly for healing—the recovery.Recovery will be difficult, almost like "walking through quicksand" difficult, if you portray your breakup as one of rejection and a lost happily ever after. When the thoughts are stuck in your head and want to be with you at 2 am, it's very simple to become trapped in this story. Conversely, conversing with members of your tribe will enable you to discover a strong perspective from which to see your story. Finding the lessons, the learning, and changing the way you perceive the experience—say, as an ending rather than a rejection—could be part of this.

3.   Writing in a journal as an emotional release.

Emotional discharge is crucial to the healing process. Writing in a journal is one approach to accomplish this because it enables you to define and record the innermost sensations and thoughts. It's not necessary to keep a journal every day for it to be effective. The healing will benefit even from a few times per week.

4.   Write as if you were speaking to a complete stranger.

Another technique to get toward healing is to write frequently about the breakup process as though speaking with a stranger about it. It not only allows for an emotional release but also promotes new perspectives and insights.

5.   Take back what has been neglected.

Gaining back a solid sense of who you are apart from the relationship is essential and will be very helpful for healing. Consider the aspects of yourself that may have been neglected throughout the relationship. Once you've identified them, think of ways to develop and nourish them.

6.   Also, enlarge them.

Find fresh methods to broaden your sense of who you are. Take up new interests, make new goals, or re-establish your orientation when you feel ready—or perhaps a little earlier. Any opportunity to interact with people who will also perceive you as your own, distinct person will actually help the healing process given that your need to connect has been interfered with.

A breakup is not a rejection; it's an end. Although it may not seem that way at first, it's crucial to keep this in mind. Finding your way back to wholeness after having your heart crushed can take some time, but you will do it. The process of getting over a broken heart involves both physical and mental healing. It is really difficult and painful since it is quite similar to getting over an addiction. Above all, keep in mind that you had qualities that were exceptional, strong, beautiful, and energetic before the relationship. There has been no change.

Breakups are as much a part of being human as breathing air and avoiding cactus licks. According to scientific research, going through a breakup activates the region of the brain connected to motivation, reward, and desires for substances like drugs and alcohol. Additionally, emotional pain activates the same brain regions as physical pain does. The bad news is that. Fortunately, things will improve.

7.   Avoid making any significant choices.

relationships, work, getting your hair cut off, and tattoos. Even though it can seem like a good idea to get "just breathe" or "live life" tattooed in times roman 120pt on your forearm, the healing process will be sluggish if you truly need these kinds of reminders

8   Remove him (or her) as a buddy on your social media accounts. Do it at once. Let's wait.

He won't post selfies with sad faces saying, "I miss you," from the places you used to visit or anything else you don't need to know. Maintaining the follow will engulf you completely. The only purpose of having him around is to make sure he isn't resuming his life too contentedly without you. And he'll be. As soon as you stop stalking people on Facebook, you'll be quite fine without him. Rip your heart out of your chest, give it to him, and tell him to squeeze it if you want to keep him as a friend. It won't hurt as bad.

9   Workout.

Though throwing "that" picture of the two of you across the room may be the only workout you feel like doing, you will feel better if you can do something more strenuous (even if it is somewhat less cathartic). The stress hormone cortisol will settle down inside of you. Exercise is one technique to extinguish the fire of cortisol.

Exercise will cause the brain to create endorphins, which are the feel-good chemicals, but you already lack them.

Therefore, you have nothing to lose. Walking will do; you don't have to build up a sweat. However, there is a warning: If the action entails leisurely passing by his home or climbing up the stormwater pipe to peer inside his window,that's called stalking !

10.   **Maintain relationships with loved ones —**

the genuine ones. not the ones who haven't been in touch with you since the last crisis. The real ones who, because you used the last clean plate three days ago, will watch "Love Actually" with you for the 37th time while you eat microwaved Indian food from the dubious plastic container it arrived in last night. A breakup hurts so badly because it plays havoc with our innate desire to connect with other people. Even if you can't be with the one person you want to be with, spending time with your tribe will satisfy your desire for connection and provide an urgent oxytocin boost (the happy hormone)You have been absent. And those true pals? Before telling you they've scheduled for the two of you to take salsa dancing lessons to get you out of the home, they'll turn on the dishwasher as you head out the door. Avoid arguing. Do it now. It's likely that you are beginning to have a week-long temper.

Nothing that makes you think of him should be in your bedroom, including fresh linens, pajamas, and scented candles. Get rid of everything that reminds you of your losses. After that, convince yourself that it wasn't there, so you haven't lost it. If not, he would be as well. Throw off those faded photos of the two of you at your almost-but-not-quite spring wedding, gazing longingly at the buffet or each other. Keep your Pinterest board titled "OMG My Wedding Yay," nonetheless. One day it will still be helpful. if you so desire. You'll recognize that it just won't be with him, and that's okay. Stop dozing off on the couch in your pajamas, too.

You're working hard. You already have plenty to worry about; you don't need to become ill on top of it all. Give your body the things it requires to work. Eat regularly and healthfully. Of course, a bucket of fried chicken every now and again will pleasure the crowd. Always use moderation. or with a tasty, crispy coating.

CHAPTER 5 Children With Your Ex?

Getting over a long-term relationship can be challenging, whether you're divorcing your spouse, getting your marriage dissolved, or splitting up with your lover. It can be particularly difficult to heal your emotional scars if you have children with your partner. You must maintain your strength for your kids and assist them in resolving their emotions rather than focusing just on your requirements and sentiments. So long as you maintain a positive attitude, breaking up with a long-term partner is achievable.

Allow for feelings

Allow yourself to experience any emotions you are having as a result of your relationship ending, including rage, fear, sadness, guilt, and anger. Don't disparage your ex in front of the kids, though. Keep any critical remarks you may have about your ex-partner to yourself, or make them in front of a counselor or sibling who is also an adult. Your children are already dealing with a challenging situation. Kids feel forced to take sides when you disparage your ex.

Make choices to complete the split.

Away from the kids, tie up any loose ends in your marriage, such as allocating assets or paying off debts. In front of the kids, refrain from arguing or arguing over these kinds of things. Consider engaging a mediator to help if you can't come to an agreement so that things don't get messy and heated.

Reach out For Assistance

Request assistance from close friends, family members, and neighbors. Ask your friends and family to share childcare responsibilities, run errands, or take turns driving to give you more time to focus on your own problems. Make contact with your family and friends. For instance, ask your parents to spend a weekend with you and your children, invite a friend and her kids to lunch, or take the kids shopping with their aunt and cousins.

Make time for yourself

Recognize that you and your kids will need some time to heal from your lengthy relationship. To accept the end of your relationship, don't rush yourself or your kids. You are all allowed to mourn the loss for however long it takes.

Avoid entering a new relationship right away. Your kids probably won't be ready to see you with someone other than their dad immediately away, despite the allure of starting a new romance to mend a shattered heart. Before exposing your kids to a new spouse or date, you should ideally wait at least six months after your separation.

Keep Things Peaceful

When it comes to creating a visitation schedule that satisfies everyone's demands, work together with your ex. If you and your ex can't come to an understanding on some issues, consider professional mediation. Due of your continued resentment toward your ex, do not attempt to restrict visitation. If you and your ex can't get along in front of the kids during visitation, think about having a friend or family help with drop-off and pick-up.

Make a Regular Schedule

Keep the same routine every day. Keep your daily routine mostly the same as it was before the separation to provide yourself and your kids a sense of familiarity and security. Consider continuing to attend work every day, driving your kids to extracurricular activities, and maintaining the same bedtimes as you did with your ex. Your kids benefit from your steadiness during a time when their lives are in a state of upheaval.

Aid Your Children with the Transition

Prepare logical and truthful responses to inquiries. Your children can inquire about upcoming holidays, events at school, or living arrangements. You'll need to put on a brave face for your kids and give them an honest response, even though you may not want to consider spending holidays apart from your spouse. Make it obvious that the children are not the focus of the divorce and that both parents adore them without condition. Your kids require assurances that they will be protected and loved.

Aid Your Children with the Transition

Prepare logical and truthful responses to inquiries. Your children can inquire about upcoming holidays, events at school, or living arrangements. You'll need to put on a brave face for your kids and give them an honest response, even though you may not want to consider spending holidays apart from your spouse. Make it obvious that the children are not the focus of the divorce and that both parents adore them without condition. Your kids require assurances that they will be protected and loved.

It's unlikely that you ever intended to raise a child with your ex-partner. However, if you and your spouse split up when your child is still very young, you'll need to figure out a solution so you can continue being parents during a critical period.

It can be extremely traumatic to end a long-term relationship, especially if there is a child involved. As you're still reeling from the shock of the breakup, you can be experiencing any number of feelings, including sadness, anger, remorse, regret, and relief. Additionally, while you may require assistance to get through it, you must bear in mind that this period in your child's life is more crucial than others.It may be helpful to seek outside assistance if you feel stuck, either in the form of relationship counseling or individual therapy. Find out what support is offered nearby by speaking with your doctor or asking at the children's center in your community. It can be challenging to move on when your feelings are still so raw.

A critical period for your child's emotional development occurs during the first three years of life. Be mindful that overnight stays in two different houses can hinder your child's emotional development if you are co-parenting with your ex. Even if you might both want the child to live with you, you might need to put your needs above your own desires. Focus on giving your child continuity and consistency rather than focusing on fairness between you and your ex.You'll need to work together and preserve a positive co-parenting relationship to do this. Even if you no longer want to be together, put your disagreements aside and make sure that your child has access to the love and care of both parents .

favorable co-parenting

By continuing to have a good relationship with your ex, you can assist your child in adjusting to your separation. Your child just needs you both to be there for them; they don't care who was at fault or who is hurting the most. Even though it may seem counterintuitive, a good relationship with your ex might really be beneficial for your child's emotional growth.

Further assistance

If you're having trouble getting along with your ex, like many other parents in your circumstances, you can feel unable to make any changes. But since change must begin somewhere, you might as well be the first.

Get rid of whatever grudges you may have, and resist the urge to point the finger at your partner. You can initiate the first constructive change. Even though it can take some perseverance, you can begin to influence your co-parenting arrangement to become the supportive force that your child needs.

CHAPTER 6 Turning Your Break-up Loss Into A Blessing

Relationships are difficult. We have no power over them. We cannot assure you that they will be successful.

Actually, when you stop to think about it, there isn't much that we actually know about relationships. Relationships, however, are not taught in any schools. The only "blueprint" of relationships most of us have is that of our parents, which is frequently not something we can (or should) imitate.

Therefore, the majority of us are not only overcome by the pain and sense of loss that follow one of the most difficult relationship events, a breakup, but we also lack the means to process this trauma and begin our path toward healing.

Try to focus on the positives.

When a relationship ends, we frequently focus on the negative aspects, such as how the other person wounded us or how they didn't make us happy in the first place.

Don't be sorry for the joyful times you enjoyed. Recognize that despite the connection not developing the way you may have hoped, you still benefited from it. You've at least gained some insight into who you are, and you can now use that information to advance yourself.

To dance, you need a partner. Consequently, whatever occurred in your relationship was the outcome of two individuals, not one, and their accountability. In other words, both of you started the relationship, and both of you failed to maintain it for x, y, or z reasons. Despite your best efforts, there are many aspects of a relationship that we are powerless to influence or alter.

Therefore, refrain from blaming yourself.

It takes however long it needs to heal. Don't put pressure on yourself because you feel you are still dealing with your ex-hurt partner's or feelings after six months or a year has passed. Everyone processes a breakup in their own special way. Simply said, this is yours.

A detrimental thought pattern is believing that the other person, the one who started the split, is not currently going through a difficult moment. Moreover, it is untrue.

For years, I organized divorce support groups, and I can assure you that both those who started the divorce and those who were divorced were present, suffering the same sorrow. Every loss we endure in life is agonizing. Don't thus assume that someone else "has it easy."

Having stated that...

You shouldn't contrast your journey after a split with your ex's. They can be doing well or not. They might have left and created a new family, or they might not have. Your travel shouldn't be affected by this anymore. It's time to concentrate more than ever before.

You shouldn't contrast your experience after a breakup with your ex's. They can be doing well or not. They might have left and created a new family, or they might not have. Your travel shouldn't be affected by this anymore. It's of more importance to put yourself first.

You undoubtedly acquired shared routines and habits if you and your partner have been dating for a time. This is the time to figure out how to "fill-in the gaps" the other person has left and discover who you are without them.

These routines may have defined your life up until this point.

Instead of concentrating on what your ex-partner, your family, or even society may believe would be best, focus on what you need and what makes you feel better.

reestablish your relationships' trust

It's pretty typical in the beginning to feel like you don't want to be with anyone, especially if the split has left you feeling extremely hurt. feeling that your faith in interpersonal interactions has been shaken. However, by going through this drawn-out and challenging process, allowing yourself to grieve, to recover, to pick up the pieces, and to reconnect with yourself once more, you'll learn to reestablish your faith in the most crucial individual: you.

And ultimately, you'll be asked to give that trust to someone else (and only you can decide when that time will be). By concentrating on oneself, as we discussed earlier, and remaining single for a while to ascertain what drives you,And what you truly need.

CHAPTER 7 Signs You Are Almost Over Your Ex

A breakup is similar to surviving a car accident. Sometimes it's just a minor collision that can be corrected. But occasionally, it's a terrible accident that absolutely wrecks your heart. Whatever the extent of your personal wounds, breakups can be traumatic and drastically alter your life. And we must navigate them alone. However, with enough time, the most agonizing agony, which you believed would never cease, begins to lessen.

You don't think about your ex as much every day. You eventually stop thinking about him or her at all. You've healed yourself and licked your wounds. You no longer think about the mess you've made; instead, you consider your new objectives. You finally put your head on your pillow one day at midnight,and you no longer have any thought of your ex.

Love's splinter finally broke off while you were preoccupied with living your life. You suddenly become aware of all the indicators that your relationship with your ex is gone.

1. You don't have to die inside when you look at couples.

2. You are completely content with returning home alone.

3. You see a familiar face, at most, in a photo of your ex rather than the love of your life.

4. You stop checking certain social media platforms compulsively.

5. You actually feel relieved when your ex finds new love.

6. You've stopped daydreaming about reuniting. In its place, you now picture your wedding day with an unidentified bride or husband.

7. You no longer feel the pain, and you choose to be happy every day (it turns out that feeling nothing at all is sometimes the best feeling).

8. You stop sobbing yourself to sleep.

9. You don't think about your ex when you wake up or fall asleep.

10. You can enjoy the sweetness of the memories you have of your relationship without getting stung, just like honey after bees have left the hive.

11. You're not holding out for an impossibly delayed text.

12. You find the journey itself to be more exciting than the "happy ending" in movies and stories.

13. You understand it's acceptable to occasionally feel a little sad that this person is no longer in your life, but you're also no longer in that relationship

14. You notice a little bit of your boyfriend or girlfriend in everyone you come into contact with throughout the day (the newspaper-handing guy who always smiles at you in the morning is your morning beau; you fall in love when the 7-Eleven cashier bids you good night).

15. While you're willing to look for a new partner, you're not in a hurry.

16. You feel powerful. You feel like Hercules after he has overcome his 12 labors because you have made it through all five phases of mourning. You've served your time, and you are aware that everything is possible if you put your mind to it.

17. You give finding love less attention than your career, hobbies, family, and friends.

18. Since you are no longer thinking about your ex, activities are no longer distractions. They are items.

19. You are able to listen to both love and breakup songs without getting emotional.

20. Rather than being angry, you're optimistic.

21. Your ex isn't the first person you think to call when amazing or bizarre things happen to you.

22. You don't pretend your pillows are your ex when you cuddle them.

23. You've come to terms with the fact that it's preferable to be single and content than unhappy in a relationship.

24. When you mention or hear your ex's name, your eyes don't light up. It sounds like you're discussing a distant pal if you even mention your ex-lover.

25. Your past with your ex becomes less and less real; they become more and more of a ghost in your mind.

26. When you consider Halloween costumes, no couples come to mind.

27. In fact, you're okay with spending the holidays alone.

28. You no longer perceive the movie theater as a danger zone for lovers. You may travel alone, with friends, family, or relatives.

29. Romantic films are once again fair game. You're not Elle Woods anymore, hurling candy and yelling "LIAR!" at every corny scene.

30. You would choose to focus on your work over the arms of a rebound.

31. You stop caring how big his d*ck or her boobs are. You'd rather find the ideal individual than a package.

CHAPTER 8 The Beginning Of A New Relationship

Once bit, twice shy. The adage holds true in relationships as well, particularly when one has soured and resulted in a breakup. As the world around you implodes, you gradually come to the realization that you must ascend. Even with a great support system, you can only help yourself succeed. When you're ready, you might soon meet new people and even discover someone interesting. Then what? How do you approach a new situation? Find out by reading on.

Think ahead

Anything in life should inspire you to look forward rather than back. Give yourself a chance if you have found someone who you find intriguing enough to think about dating for the simple reason that you deserve it. Consider having fun and letting the past go. Think of it as a new stage in your life rather than as a replacement for the prior individual.

Avoid making analogies.

Although it's easier said than done, you must really try. Because each individual is unique, the way your ex handled things will unavoidably differ from the way your current interest does. Try to avoid comparing the two; doing so can only lead to tragedy.

Observe the new person for a while.

You don't have to make a decision regarding the new applicant right away. Despite the passage of time, the split is still fresh in your mind and may affect how you perceive the new person. Give him some space, accept his meetup requests, and go out with him with the purpose of having fun. You will become comfortable with the concept after a few dates, at which point you can make an objective decision about how you want this new relationship to develop.

Stop thinking about seeing your ex again.

Due to your intense affections for someone, you frequently find yourself thinking about them again and again. Remind yourself of the problems that led to your split in the first place, reason with yourself, and be practical. Those problems went unaddressed, and it's likely that they won't ever be. It's preferable if you quit considering the possibilities of reconciling with your ex. It should go without saying that you should cut him off if necessary, even by blocking him on social media.

Consider the advantages of the new hire.

That's what will keep you two motivated! He is reciprocating, which is one of the reasons you found him attractive. He must possess some admirable attributes that you must observe and allow shine so that you may be sure you are on the correct path. Pay attention to the minute details and how he handles them or what he does for you. While you can, take advantage of the attention.

CONCLUSION